HISTORY IN LITERATURE

THE STORY BEHIND...

TONI MORRISON'S
THE BLUEST EYE

Mary Colson

Heinemann Library
Chicago, Illinois

Customer Service 888–454–2279

Visit our website at www.heinemannraintree.com

Designed by Richard Parker and Tinstar Design
Printed in China by Leo Paper Group

11 10 09 08 07
10 9 8 7 6 5 4 3 2 1

Library of Congress Cataloging-in-Publication Data
Colson, Mary.
  The story behind Toni Morrison's The Bluest Eye / Mary
Colson.   p. cm. -- (History in literature)
  Includes bibliographical references and index.
  ISBN 1-4034-8212-8 (lib. bdg.)
  1. Morrison, Toni. Bluest eye--Juvenile literature. 2. Morrison,
Toni--Juvenile literature. 3. United States--Race
relations--History--Juvenile literature. I. Title. II. Series.

  PS3563.08749 B5525 2006
  813/.54 22
                            2006004662

Acknowledgments
The publishers would like to thank the following for permission to reproduce photographs: "Cover", from The Bluest Eye by Toni Morrison, copyright © 1993 by Toni Morrison. Used by permission of Plume, an imprint of Penguin Group (USA) Inc p. 39; Advertising Archives pp. 26, 31, 35; Bridgeman Art Library p. 15 (Private Collection); CORBIS pp. 10, 11, p. 21 (Annie Griffiths Belt), 13, 18, 20, 22, 25, 27, 29, 32, 38, 45 (Bettmann), 36 (Bradley Smith), 23 (Flip Schulke), 6 (Joseph Schwartz), 41 (Reuters), 47 (Roger Ressmeyer), 43 (Tom & Dee Ann McCarthy); Empics pp. 16, 24, 40, 46, 49 (AP); Getty Images pp. 9 (Charles Hewitt), 37 (Ernst Haas), 33 (Frank Driggs Collection), 42 (Frederick M. Brown), 30 (George Eastman House/Lewis W. Hine), 28 (John Kobal Foundation), 14 (MPI), 17 (New York Times Co.), 48 (Terry O'Neill), 12 (Time Life Pictures/Fritz Goro), 44 (Time Magazine/ Time & Life Pictures); Magnum Photos p. 7 (Danny Lyon); MARY EVANS p. 8 (STEVE RUMNEY COLLECTION); Collection of the Norman Rockwell Museum, Stockbridge, Massachusetts. Reproduced by permission of the Norman Rockwell Family Agency, Inc. p. 19; Ohio Historical Society p. 34; Rex Features p. 4.

Excerpts from The Bluest Eye by Toni Morrison, © 1970 renewed 1988 by Toni Morrison. Afterword © 1993 by Toni Morrison, used by permission of Alfred A Knopf, a division of Random House, Inc.

Cover photograph of Toni Morrison reproduced with permission of Getty Images/Todd Pitt.
Background photos reproduced with permission of Getty Images/Charles Hewitt; Photos.com.

The publishers would like to thank Professor Marc Conner for his assistance in the preparation of this book.

Every effort has been made to contact copyright holders of any material reproduced in this book. Any omissions will be rectified in subsequent printings if notice is given to the publisher.

Disclaimer
All the Internet addresses (URLs) given in this book were valid at the time of going to press. However, due to the dynamic nature of the Internet, some addresses may have changed or ceased to exist since publication. While the author and publishers regret any inconvenience this may cause readers, no responsibility for any such changes can be accepted by either the author or the publishers.

Contents

Some words are shown in bold, **like this**. You can find out what they mean by looking in the glossary.

Writing from Experience

Born Chloe Anthony Wofford in 1931 in Lorain, Ohio, Toni Morrison is one of the world's most celebrated writers. Growing up in the 1930s and 1940s, she experienced firsthand both **prejudice** and poverty. She later used these experiences in her acclaimed first novel, *The Bluest Eye*, which was published in 1970. It is the tragic story of eleven-year-old Pecola Breedlove, a young African-American girl who prays "each night without fail" for blue eyes. She thinks blue eyes will make her beautiful and therefore make her life better. Pecola believes she is ugly because she and her community base their **ideals** of beauty on whiteness.

Toni Morrison has never been afraid of tackling challenging issues and subjects. Throughout her work, she has tried to recreate African-American experiences and to portray the characters of African-American communities accurately.

CHANGING IDENTITY

*In 1949 Chloe Wofford entered Howard University in Washington, D.C. It was there that she changed her name from "Chloe" to "Toni" because people found "Chloe" hard to pronounce. She continued her studies at Cornell University, where she met and married Harold Morrison. By 1958 she was back at Howard teaching students, some of whom would later become famous writers and civil rights **activists**, including the poet Amiri Baraka and the writer Claude Brown. Brown's **autobiography**, Manchild in the Promised Land, is about the experiences of African Americans who left the **sharecropping** South for the crowded inner cities of the North and a new life and identity, just like Toni Morrison's family.*

The Great Migration saw the mass movement of thousands of African Americans from the South to the North. The Great Migration created the first large, urban African-American communities in the North, which saw its black population rise about 20 percent between 1910 and 1930.

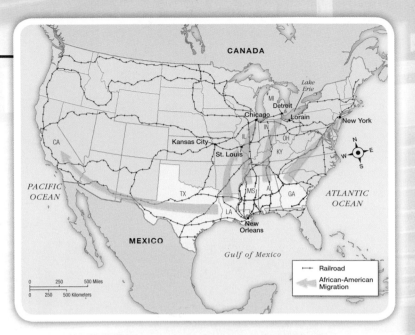

ON THE ROAD

The **Wall Street Crash** of 1929, and the **Great Depression** that followed, saw millions of Americans struggling to make ends meet. Between 1930 and 1970, four million African Americans **migrated** north in search of work. They left the South, the cotton fields, and sharecropping behind them. Toni Morrison's parents were among the first to migrate. They left their settled lives and headed to the steel town of Lorain, Ohio, in the 1920s— just as Pecola's parents do in the novel. Formerly a **sharecropper**, George Wofford, Toni's father, took a welding job. At night, he would tell his children the folktales that his father had told him.

The Bluest Eye developed out of a conversation Morrison had in elementary school with a girl who longed for blue eyes. Morrison was still thinking about this conversation in 1962 when she joined a writers' group. Although the story is set in 1941, Morrison wrote it from 1965 to 1969. This was a time of great social unrest in the United States. The country was booming economically, but alongside this wealth was a large group of people whose opportunities were limited by poor schooling, high unemployment, and society's attitudes toward them.

More than a century after slavery ended, African Americans still dreamed of equality.

During this period, widespread national protests demanded equal rights for African Americans and created an unstoppable movement for political change. Black entertainment stars gradually became part of mainstream U.S. culture, and the African-American community started to rediscover its own beauty ideals. This cultural and historical background influenced the writing of *The Bluest Eye*.

5

In the 1940s, housing was still **segregated** in the United States. In the overcrowded northern cities, African Americans arriving from the South lived in cramped, unhygienic conditions in crowded tenement blocks, such as these in Brooklyn, New York.

Writing and speaking about life

The Bluest Eye is not an autobiography. However, it is set in the town where Morrison grew up, and it is told from the point of view of a nine-year-old girl, which is the age Morrison would have been in 1941—the year the novel takes place. The novel tells not just one story, but rather interlocking stories that gradually piece together the lives of people in Pecola's community. Much of the novel is told from the perspective of Claudia MacTeer, Pecola's school friend. Like Pecola, Claudia suffers from the black community's belief in its own ugliness (compared to whiteness), but she has a loving and stable family. The MacTeer family serves as a sharp contrast to Pecola's family, the Breedloves.

Pecola's parents, Pauline and Cholly Breedlove, have a physically violent relationship that leads to their son, Sammy, running away. A depressed alcoholic, Cholly is an abusive and violent man who **rapes** his own daughter. Pecola becomes pregnant, but the baby later dies. Morrison does not justify Cholly's behavior, but does try to explain it in terms of his own lost childhood and rejection by his father.

People broken into pieces

At the start of the novel, Morrison uses a paragraph from a Dick and Jane-style reading **primer**: "Here is the house [...] here is the family," describes a fantasy white family experience. This contrasts with the **stark** horror of Pecola's situation. Pecola is a fragile child when the novel begins, and by the novel's close, her mental breakdown is complete. In an effort to be seen, Pecola "**hallucinates** a self."

In other words, her insanity reveals itself in her intense imagining that she has blue eyes and that she is "other" than what she is. She is driven insane by violence, abuse, and a desire to not be ugly anymore.

In an **afterword**, the author describes Pecola's wider community as a "shattered world," a group of people struggling to exist amid poverty and racial **discrimination**.

THE SPOKEN STORY

The writer Mildred Taylor has explained how telling stories is a key part of African-American culture and history: "By the fireside, [...] I learned a history not then written in books but one passed from generation to generation [...] From my father the storyteller I learned to respect the past, to respect my own heritage and myself." This oral, or spoken, tradition of storytelling comes from black preachers in churches in the 1800s. Traditionally, they would tell the **congregation** Bible stories out loud because few people could read. As a child, Morrison heard her own father's stories. In her writing, she reproduces African-American speech patterns, like Mrs. MacTeer's "fussing **soliloquies**" in which she complains about her lot in life: "I guess I ain't supposed to have nothing." The Bluest Eye records the kind of story not printed in reading primers. A different language is required to communicate this experience.

An African-American woman uses story and speech to stir up support during the civil rights movement, 1962.

The image problem

In the 1940s, white beauty was visible everywhere. From candy wrappers in shops to movie screens, whiteness was presented in a positive, desirable light. With few visible African-American role models, the African-American community started to believe that whiteness was superior. Morrison has called this process "self-destruction." *The Bluest Eye* explores the effects of racial self-hatred and is a story about a community searching for self-acceptance within a larger society in which white beauty is dominant. A neglected child who wants to be loved, Pecola is the person who suffers most from this. She hears of her "ugliness" from every side; at home from her mother, who remembers her as an "ugly" baby, and from the children at school, who torment her. As Morrison has explained, Pecola clings to the idea that "if those eyes of hers were different, that is to say, beautiful, she herself would be different"—and therefore loved.

Movie's golden age

In the 1930s and 1940s images of beautiful white actresses such as Greta Garbo, Jean Harlow, and Ginger Rogers filled the movie screens and **saturated** the billboards. Most popular of all at this time was a child actress named Shirley Temple (1928–), whose trademark dimples, corkscrew golden curls, and twinkling blue eyes made her a national icon.

Temple was the highest-paid child actress of her day. Singing and dancing in her movies, she starred in more than 40 films and won an Academy Award at the age of six. A multimillion dollar merchandising industry was created around her likeness, with her face printed on records, hats, dresses, mugs, and gift cards. Pecola is fixated with the Shirley Temple cup at the MacTeer house, and she drinks quarts of milk from it just to be able to stare at the image.

With milky skin and clear blue eyes, white dolls were one of the best-selling toys of the 1940s. Pecola believes that she can only become beautiful if she has blue eyes, just like the doll.

A problem of perception

Pecola's world is full of messages that whiteness and white culture are superior. Even Pecola's own mother, Pauline, prefers the little white girl whose parents she works for. Caring for the white family removes Pauline from her own family. Mrs. Breedlove was fascinated by white beauty, in particular by the movie actress Jean Harlow, saying, "The onliest time I be happy seem like was when I was in the picture show. […] I fixed my hair up like I'd seen hers." Morrison also uses the characters of Geraldine, whose son invites Pecola to play inside his house, and Maureen, a pale-skinned African-American girl who "enchanted"the whole school with her beauty, to show the racism that also exists within Pecola's black community. Both characters reject Pecola because she is "black" and "ugly."

Set in the economic hardship of the pre-World War II 1940s, and written during the social unrest of the 1960s, Morrison wrote her novel to show "how something as **grotesque** as the **demonization** of an entire race could take root inside the most delicate member of society: a child." **Internalized** racism was both deeply damaging and deeply rooted in the history of black America in the 1900s.

An Historic Agenda

The 1930s had been a time of great poverty and hardship for millions of Americans. In *The Bluest Eye*, Claudia describes African Americans at that time as living "on the hem of life," suggesting that they were on the very edge of society and unable to change anything.

A sharecropper rented a plot of land and paid for it with a percentage of the crop—sometimes as much as 50 percent of the harvest. Sharecroppers bought tools, seeds, and food from the farm owner on credit, but often had barely enough to survive.

The Great Depression and the New Deal

In 1929 the economic collapse of Wall Street shocked the United States. Overnight, businesses went bankrupt as the dollar dramatically **devalued** and millions of people lost their jobs. This marked the start of the Great Depression, which lasted for a decade. President Franklin D. Roosevelt set up a series of laws and programs called the New Deal, which stabilized the economy and created jobs—particularly factory jobs in northern states.

HARD TIMES

*The Agricultural Adjustment Act of 1933 was designed to help the farming industry, but this new law was a disaster for sharecroppers. To keep food prices high, millions of farm animals were slaughtered and the meat was wasted, which prevented it from oversupplying the market. At a time when many families could not afford food, this caused outrage. Farmers were paid by the government not to grow crops, and so sharecroppers were no longer needed. Many of these were African Americans who were forced to uproot themselves and search for work elsewhere. In the novel, Morrison uses Mrs. MacTeer's frequent rants against the New Deal to express African-American **discontent** with President Roosevelt's decisions.*

While many thought the New Deal was a great success, not everybody benefited from it. Many African-American sharecroppers and people who already lived below the poverty line found life even harder and were forced to move to find work.

The great move north

Newspapers, such as the black-owned *Chicago Defender*, urged African Americans to migrate north to towns like Lorain, Ohio, where there was a shortage of factory workers. Chicago had a direct train route from Mississippi, so it was a natural first choice for people leaving the South. In *The Bluest Eye*, Mrs. Breedlove's family has already moved from Alabama to Kentucky for work and, once she marries Cholly, the couple move again, "way up north" to Lorain. The Great Migration north tore communities and families apart. Morrison shows how some families, like the MacTeers, managed to stay strong, while the Breedloves self-destruct.

In the 1930s, millions of African-American sharecroppers moved north. There, they enjoyed more freedom and could vote freely.

Inside a Chicago slum, 1954. In her **Nobel Prize** speech of 1993, Morrison suggested that there was still a long way to go for full racial equality and **integration**. She asked writers to portray the African-American experience accurately. "Tell us [...] what it is to have no home in this place. [...] What it is to live at the edge of towns that cannot bear your company."

An equal freedom?

In January 1941, President Roosevelt delivered a State of the Union address in which he outlined the "Four Freedoms" that all people across the world should enjoy. These were freedom from want, freedom of speech, freedom to worship, and freedom from fear. Through her **narrative**, Morrison shows that, in reality, most **impoverished** African Americans did not enjoy these freedoms. The opening pages show Claudia and her sister, Frieda, as being so poor they must walk along the railroad tracks where they "fill **burlap sacks** with the tiny pieces of coal lying about." Later, we see them selling seeds and calling at "twelve-room houses that sheltered half as many families."

A CREATIVE REBIRTH

*Once African Americans reached the northern cities, a larger community meant more of a group identity. From the time of slavery until the 1960s, African-American and white culture had been officially separated. Along with schools and cafes, African Americans had their own churches, music, songs, and art. The Harlem **Renaissance**, or rebirth, of the 1920s was a key movement in changing white **perceptions** of African-American performing arts. Based in Harlem, the poet Langston Hughes was a key figure of the movement. His poem "I, Too, Sing America" uses the image of a dining table around which whites and African Americans sit and eat together. From this time onward, African-American culture began to be absorbed into **mainstream** U.S. culture.*

World War II

The Japanese attack on Pearl Harbor in 1941 led the United States to enter World War II (1939–1945). Many young black men saw the war as an opportunity to serve their country and gain greater respect. While on leave in European cities controlled by British or U.S. forces, black soldiers found that they were treated without prejudice. They could eat, drink, and sleep in the same places that white people did. However, upon returning home, black soldiers who had been willing to fight and die for their country were still not granted equal citizenship. In the afterword to *The Bluest Eye*, Morrison explains her double purpose of setting the story in the fall of 1941. In December 1941, the United States entered World War II. At the same time, Pecola's tragedy is about to be told. In both cases, Morrison has said, "something grim" is about to happen.

African-American sailor Doris "Dorie" Miller receives the Navy Cross for his heroism during the Pearl Harbor attacks. This was the first time this medal of honor had been awarded to an African-American member of the armed forces.

RISING TENSION

During World War II, thousands of jobs were created in the U.S. defense industry, but racial divisions continued. In 1943, in Mobile, Alabama, race riots broke out at the Atlanta Drydock and Shipbuilding Company following the promotion of twelve African-American shipyard workers. White workers were angry that African Americans were working alongside them, and two days of violence erupted. Events such as this show the widespread racial tension that forms The Bluest Eye's historical backdrop.

13

Outsiders

In the 1940s, racial segregation affected almost every area of daily life, from playgrounds to buses. The history of racial segregation goes back to the Jim Crow laws that existed mainly in the South and that had been enforced since 1877. This group of laws segregated whites from African Americans in various places, including restaurants, schools, and parks. Claudia and Frieda "dream" about the park they are not allowed to go in, but they have accepted living apart from whites. When Morrison explains that "black people were not allowed in the park," it is a statement of fact rather than sorrow.

The United States is a country consisting of people of different groups who have come from different countries. Often these different groups, however, were united against African Americans. Morrison has noted that the mainly white **immigrants** from many different cultures all joined together in looking down on African Americans. When Pecola goes into Mr. Yacobowski's store to buy some candy, the white immigrant shopkeeper meets her with "distaste" and "the total absence of human recognition."

Every part of life was segregated in the South. This is a store meant only for African Americans (called "coloreds" at the time), in 1925.

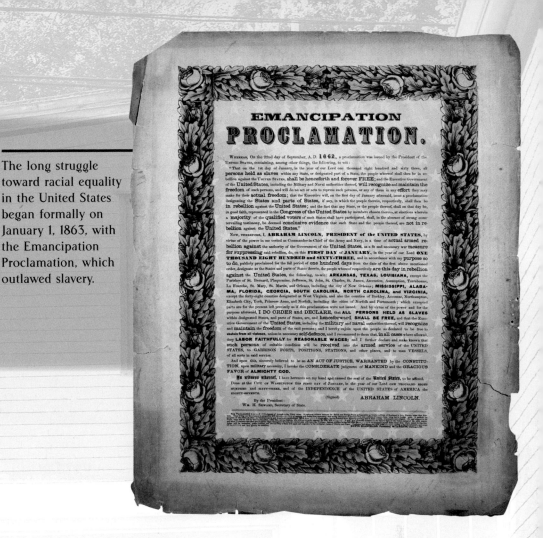

The long struggle toward racial equality in the United States began formally on January 1, 1863, with the Emancipation Proclamation, which outlawed slavery.

A place called home

In the 1940s, segregation in housing was common. States such as California gave local groups the right to say where members of certain races could live. By the time this kind of control was overturned, residential segregation patterns were established in most U.S. cities, and many remain today, with millions of African Americans still living in the poorest areas. In *The Bluest Eye*, Claudia and Frieda walk from their house to Lake Erie, marveling at the gradual change and improvements in the streets and houses as they enter white neighborhoods.

Being able to house and feed your family was a challenge for all Americans during the Depression. Morrison's main narrator, Claudia, talks about the "terror of life" that is losing your house and being "outdoors." Even as a child, Claudia knows the difference between being "put out" by a **landlord** for not paying the rent and putting oneself "outdoors." This was the case of Cholly, who has "burned up his house" and made his family homeless. With Cholly in a **workhouse**, the authorities place Pecola with the MacTeers until her family can be reunited.

Lynching is the illegal execution of an accused person by a mob. Lynching was originally a system of punishment used by whites against African-American slaves. However, whites who protested against this were also in danger of being lynched.

Deep divisions

In the 1930s and 1940s, racial violence and **persecution** continued. Whites often attacked African Americans while the authorities "looked the other way." Racist groups targeted and **lynched** African Americans. Lynch mobs were most active in the early 1900s, but they were still claiming victims in the 1940s and after. Lynching victims became a powerful image of race relations in the United States.

Written by Abel Meeropol, and later sung by Billie Holiday, the poem "Strange Fruit" is about lynching:

"Black bodies swinging in the southern breeze, strange fruit hanging from the poplar trees."

By the time Morrison wrote *The Bluest Eye*, she was able to be more open and political in her use of the lynching image. Maureen Peel, the pretty new girl at Claudia's school, is described as having beautiful hair "braided into two lynch ropes." Morrison wanted to shock readers by putting together images of beauty and cruelty.

THE COLOR-LINE

*One of the most influential writers of the early 1900s, and a founder of the **National Association for the Advancement of Colored People (NAACP)**, was W. E. B. Du Bois. In 1903 he published a groundbreaking collection of essays on race entitled The Souls of Black Folk, which describe how African Americans lived in U.S. society. Du Bois was against all forms of segregation and famously summarized American life by saying, "The problem of the twentieth century is the problem of the **color-line**." In The Bluest Eye, Morrison shows that the "color-line" is not limited to simple differences between black and white, but rather divisions exist within the African-American community itself.*

All areas of cultural life were officially segregated in the 1940s and 1950s. Public areas had a different entrance for African-American patrons (see right). It was through theater and music, however, that African-American culture became popular with white America and African-American artists gradually enjoyed wider appeal.

REWRITING RACISM

*Some of the first great African-American novels sprang from the misery of the 1930s and 1940s. With the publication of Native Son in 1940, Richard Wright was among the first black writers to achieve literary fame and fortune. Like Morrison, he was a child of a sharecropper and spent his early years on a **plantation** in Mississippi. Wright wanted to portray African Americans accurately to white readers in the hope of destroying the **myths** surrounding race.*

*Ralph Ellison's 1952 masterpiece, Invisible Man, describes a black man's **quest** for identity and a place in a hostile world. The narrator is "invisible" in a symbolic sense. People refuse to see him, just as Pecola is overlooked in The Bluest Eye. Like Morrison's novel, Ellison's story deals with the difficult issue of **incest**.*

A Hundred Years of Struggle

For more than a century, African Americans had been protesting to gain full rights as U.S. citizens. The civil rights movement involved many different organizations, including the NAACP, the Congress of Racial Equality, the Southern Christian Leadership Conference, and various women's groups. Far from being united, the groups all had different goals and methods. In 1964 and 1965, the **Civil Rights Act** and the **Voting Rights Act** finally made all U.S. citizens equal according to the law. But to achieve these results, an intense decade of protest that affected every part of U.S. society was necessary. Toni Morrison witnessed these events and watched communities being torn apart by racism. It was during this time of severe racial tension that she was inspired to write *The Bluest Eye*.

In 1957 in Little Rock, Arkansas, nine black students tried to enter the Little Rock Central High School. The state governor, Orval Faubus, ordered National Guardsmen to prevent the students from going in. In a key response in favor of civil rights, President Dwight D. Eisenhower sent 1,000 troops to protect black students on their way to school.

On November 14, 1960, six-year-old Ruby Bridges became a symbol of the ongoing struggle for integrated education in the South. Surrounded by federal marshals, she crossed angry protest lines and entered a New Orleans school that had previously only been open to whites. Many white parents withdrew their children in protest, and Ruby was taught by herself for a year. The painting above by Norman Rockwell is called *The Problem We All Live With* (1964). It portrays Ruby's brave walk to school. In 2004 Morrison wrote a nonfiction account of the desegregation of education in *Remember: The Journey to School Integration*.

Community in crisis

From the 1950s to 1960s, the continuing lack of economic equality led to resentment and then to racial violence between whites and African Americans. In the 1940s to 1960s, African Americans earned on average between 40 and 60 percent of the average white income. Employment and a career are part of any self-image. Pauline Breedlove works and has a defined identity and role within the white family she works for. In the white home, Pauline feels "power," but ironically, she does not feel the same in her own home. The economic contrast between the white home and the Breedloves' is too great to overcome, so Pauline neglects her own. Members of Pauline's family become "afterthoughts."

"THE PROBLEM WE ALL LIVE WITH"

The Nobel Prize-winning writer John Steinbeck was passing through New Orleans in 1960 and wrote a description of watching Ruby go to school, in his book *Travels with Charley*:

The big marshals stood her on the curb and a jangle of jeering shrieks went up from behind the barricades. The little girl did not look at the howling crowd but from the side the whites of her eyes showed like those of a frightened faun.

In May 1963, riot police spray water canons into protesters who were angry about continued segregation.

The search for an identity

As the civil rights movement gathered **momentum**, desegregation in schools became one of the largest battlegrounds of the struggle. Morrison herself had studied at the black college Howard University in the late 1940s. She returned there to teach from 1957 to 1964, while activists continued their protests against segregation all over the country.

The movement was not just a fight for equal rights, but also a search for an African-American identity. It aimed to **empower** people, like Cholly Breedlove, who felt that they would never belong. Tensions ran high and often turned violent as protesters across the country let out their frustrations about segregation.

A loss of male self

Although *The Bluest Eye* deals primarily with the effects of racism on women, the men in the novel are also **disempowered**. They often take out the resulting frustrations on female victims. Cholly Breedlove is an example of this loss of identity. He has been made powerless by his poverty and lacks self-respect. He is a man who has suffered neglect and rejection from his own father. As a teenager, Cholly was interrupted by two white men while he had sex with a young woman. They then forced him to continue while they stood by and watched.

Cholly **displaced** his hatred for the two men onto his girlfriend. The humiliation Cholly feels damages his sense of masculinity. He is described as "small, black, helpless." Unable to direct his anger toward the two men because they are "big, white, armed," he becomes angry instead toward his girlfriend. This same anger is later directed toward both Pauline and Pecola.

THE PEN IS MIGHTIER THAN THE SWORD

There are more than 100 Historically Black Colleges and Universities (HBCU) in the United States, all of which were established before 1964 for the education of African-American students. Before the creation of HBCUs, African Americans were almost always excluded from higher-education opportunities. Morrison attended and taught at Howard University. An HBCU, Howard was one of nine black colleges founded immediately following the Civil War (1861–1865). Mainly situated in southern and eastern states, HBCUs boast many prestigious former students, including Andrew Young Jr., the former mayor of Atlanta, W. E. B. Du Bois, and Oprah Winfrey. One of Morrison's students, Amiri Baraka, became an award-winning poet and playwright. His work reflects the pain of prejudice and of living in a hostile society. Baraka helped to start the Black Arts movement. He formed a theater company in Harlem, and he wrote for many magazines throughout the 1960s. Artists such as Baraka wanted to protest and create change through their work, not through violence. Baraka said, "I see art as a weapon, and a weapon of revolution."

The valedictorian for a Howard University graduating class (left) celebrates with a friend before their commencement ceremony. She is going on to start her career in finance, on Wall Street.

Turning point

On December 1, 1955, in Montgomery, Alabama, Rosa Parks's refusal to give up her bus seat for a white man led to her arrest. In protest, 50,000 people **boycotted** the city buses for more than a year, until seating was finally integrated. The boycott brought worldwide sympathy to the cause and, in 1956, the U.S. Supreme Court ruled that segregation on buses was illegal. With a new belief in the power of protest and the movement, the stage was set for a civil rights leader to emerge.

Martin Luther King Jr. (1929–1968)

Born in Atlanta in 1929, Martin Luther King Jr. would become the most famous civil rights leader of all time. He became a minister in Montgomery, Alabama, and led the bus boycott. With his Southern Christian Leadership Conference, King led mass demonstrations in Birmingham, Alabama. There, clashes between unarmed black demonstrators and police armed with dogs and fire hoses generated newspaper headlines throughout the world. King reached out to people on the "hem of life," like the MacTeers and the Breedloves, and shared his vision of a "promised land" for all Americans.

A TIME TO ACT

The time has come for this Nation to fulfill its promise. The events in Birmingham and elsewhere have so increased the cries for equality that no city or State or legislative body can prudently choose to ignore them.

—President John F. Kennedy, June 11, 1963.

In August 1963, thousands of civil rights protesters marched past the Capitol building in Washington, D.C.

"Let freedom ring..."

On August 28, 1963, more than 200,000 demonstrators gathered at the Lincoln Memorial, in Washington, D.C., to take part in the March for Jobs and Freedom. An **alliance** of civil rights organizations planned the march to show that a gap existed between the supposed rights of American democracy and the everyday experience of African Americans. This was a movement begun during the Depression. It grew out of frustration at the New Deal and how it overlooked black needs. During the march, Martin Luther King Jr. delivered his "I Have a Dream" speech. The march was successful, and the administration of President John F. Kennedy made a commitment to passing a civil rights law.

Different ways to change

Mahatma Gandhi was the inspiration for King's policy of nonviolence. Born in India in 1869, Gandhi came to world attention in the 1930s for leading peaceful protest marches against British rule in India, which came to an end in 1947, a year before his death. Gandhi also inspired others.

Stokely Carmichael, a former student of Morrison's, followed Gandhi's teachings. In 1966 he became national chairman of the **Student Nonviolent Coordinating Committee**. Two years later, frustrated by the lack of change, he joined the Black Panther Party. The Black Panther Party rejected Gandhi's and King's policy of nonviolence and taught members that armed self-defense was acceptable. Jailed many times for his protests, Carmichael's rallying cry was "black power!"

On a Sunday morning in September 1963, the **Ku Klux Klan (KKK)** bombed a Baptist church in Birmingham, Alabama. Inside the church, five young African-American girls were changing into their choir robes. The bomb exploded, killing four of the five girls and injuring twenty people. The girls who were murdered were eleven-year-old Denise McNair (top right) and (anti-clockwise from top left) fourteen-year-olds Addie Mae Collins, Carole Robertson, and Cynthia Wesley. The murder of these four young girls led to national outrage.

By 1964 there was enough political momentum for the Civil Rights Act to pass, despite the assassination of its great champion, President Kennedy, the previous year. The act outlawed segregation in places such as movie theaters, restaurants, and hotels. It banned **gender** or race discrimination in employment and ended segregation in libraries, schools, and parks. Over twenty years after Claudia and Frieda dreamed of entering the white park, the law had finally been changed.

TOGETHER AND EQUAL?

On July 2, 1964, President Lyndon B. Johnson signed the Civil Rights Act into law. The Civil Rights Act overturned decades of "separate but equal" policies, and African Americans and white Americans at last had equal status under the law.

*"We believe that all men are created equal. Yet many are denied equal treatment. We believe that all men have certain **unalienable** rights. Yet many Americans do not enjoy those rights.*

We believe that all men are entitled to the blessings of liberty. Yet millions are being deprived of those blessings—not because of their own failures, but because of the color of their skin. [...] But it cannot continue."

– President Lyndon B. Johnson

Inspiration from life

A year after the Civil Rights Act was signed, Morrison began writing *The Bluest Eye* as a novel—developing it from a short story she had quickly written. She put a lifetime's worth of inequality, discrimination, and **vulnerability** as an African American into this novel. By focusing on young female characters, Morrison shows us the experience of black women in all aspects of life.

RACE RIOTS

*From 1919 to the present day, riots have marked racial tensions throughout the United States. In Chicago, in 1919, a riot broke out after a black youth was killed in white "territory." During the week of violence that followed, 38 people died. Riots in Detroit in 1943 and 1967 damaged the city's economy for years afterward. In Philadelphia, in August 1964, tensions rose between black residents and the police, and violence erupted. Three days of rioting led to hundreds of injuries, arrests, and **allegations** of police brutality. In the days following the assassination of Martin Luther King Jr., on April 4, 1968, riots erupted in more than 100 cities across 28 states. President Johnson sent out 20,000 regular troops and 24,000 National Guardsmen to calm the confrontations, and many areas enforced **curfews**. By April 23, 46 people had died, 2,600 were injured, and more than 20,000 people had been arrested.*

Identifying with Beauty

At the heart of Pecola's story is a search for identity and a desire to be seen. She is caught between a Shirley Temple ideal of white beauty and the reality of the violence and neglect that surrounds her. In the novel, a narrator explains that Pecola will "never know her own beauty." Forever overlooked, the young girl becomes a symbol of racial identity crisis. Toni Morrison says that her novel is about the "damage" that results from trying to adopt a standard of beauty that is "alien" or foreign to one's own culture. Morrison was "writing about beauty, miracles, and self-images, about the way in which people can hurt each other, about whether or not one is beautiful." Pecola, Pauline, and even Claudia and Frieda are all affected by the white beauty ideal and its failure to acknowledge black beauty.

Meet the girl men want to kiss

Advertisements in the 1940s were dominated by images of white women and children. The slogans, such as the one for Tangee lipstick, played on the idea that white features were more attractive. Pecola and Claudia are surrounded by examples of white beauty. Claudia rejects these ideals, but Pecola believes the ads and desires white features so much that she goes insane.

SWEET TEMPTATION

Even when she is buying candy, Pecola cannot avoid the reach of white beauty publicity. Invented in 1915, the Mary Jane candy wrapper has a picture of a white child with blond hair and blue eyes. Pecola finds this image beautiful, and it reinforces her idea of what beauty is. As she eats the candy, in her mind she is transformed into the white ideal: "To eat the candy is somehow to eat the eyes, eat Mary Jane. Love Mary Jane. Be Mary Jane."

A theory of race

In the 1800s in France, an **aristocrat**, the Comte de Gobineau, wrote a book about the inequality of the human races. His theory, which Morrison quotes from in *The Bluest Eye*, claims that all civilizations come from the white race and that "none can exist without its help." This theory of white **supremacy** had far-reaching effects. At the time Morrison was growing up and millions of African Americans were being left out of President Roosevelt's New Deal, racists in **Nazi** Germany were using parts of de Gobineau's theory to persecute Jewish people.

The color of cleanliness?

In the novel, whiteness is constantly associated with beauty and cleanliness. Even the white Mary Jane figure on Pecola's candy wrapper stares at her "out of a world of clean comfort." The African-American characters in the novel who have white, middle-class values are obsessed with cleanliness. Geraldine—whose son invites Pecola to play—and Mrs. Breedlove are very concerned with house cleaning, although Mrs. Breedlove cleans only the house of her white employees. Cleaning her own home is not a priority. Geraldine, on the other hand, takes great pride in her house and its presentation. However, this obsession with cleaning leads both women to be cruel and cold, particularly toward Pecola. The adult Claudia notes of Pecola that the whole community "felt so wholesome after we cleaned ourselves on her. We were so beautiful when we stood astride her ugliness."

Pecola's family is very different from the typical image of a white family from the 1940s. Her parents fight and yell and do not pay enough attention to her. Throughout *The Bluest Eye,* Morrison shows the reader how different Pecola's life is from the white ideal.

In the 1930s, the actress Jean Harlow became known as the "original blond bombshell." A huge sex symbol, Harlow started a craze for platinum blond hair that continues to this day. Pecola's mother, Pauline, goes to the movies over and over again to watch Harlow and tries to wear her hair and makeup in the same way.

Screen beauties

Ideas of beauty were most widely popularized in the movies. By the mid-1940s, the white glamour of Hollywood movie stars, models, and beauty queens set the beauty standard. White child actresses, such as Shirley Temple and Jane Withers, were adored by African-American girls like Pecola and Claudia, while Jean Harlow and Greta Garbo were admired by African-American women like Pauline. In *The Bluest Eye*, the Breedlove family members have a strong feeling that they are ugly. Morrison suggests that this is due to historical prejudice against the appearance of African Americans and that society has been saturated with images of white beauty.

Roles and restrictions

In the 1940s and 1950s, it was almost impossible for an African-American actress to have a long-running career in Hollywood because appropriate roles were not being written. As a result, there were very few African-American role models in the beauty or entertainment industry, and therefore few advertisements featured famous black faces. Gradually this changed, but only when the roles for African-American performers expanded from their playing maids, slaves, or African natives. The first African American to win a Supporting Actress Oscar was Hattie McDaniel, for her role as a slave in *Gone with the Wind* (1939).

THE BLACK PRESS

In The Bluest Eye, Pauline reads about Jean Harlow in a magazine that would have been aimed at a white reader. In 1945, four years after the novel is set, John H. Johnson launched one of the first magazines for African Americans. Ebony included articles and stories about African-American successes and was modeled on white lifestyle magazines, such as Life. For the first time, national corporations featured black models driving cars and drinking soft drinks on the advertising pages. With the success of Ebony, Johnson's publishing empire grew and he launched Jet magazine. In 1955 Jet published a photograph of a young black boy, in an open coffin, who was murdered because he was alleged to have whistled at a white woman. After that, both Ebony and Jet became involved in the civil rights struggle, publishing political articles about racial divisions in the United States.

Lena Horne and Dorothy Dandridge were two of the most popular and highly paid African-American performers of the 1940s and 1950s. Horne was a singer, dancer, and actress, and the NAACP helped her to get a long-term movie studio contract, the first African American to do so. The color barrier meant that her early movie roles were limited and, as Horne said, "I didn't get much of a chance to act." Dorothy Dandridge was more successful. She was the first black woman to appear on the cover of *Life* magazine, and, in 1954, she became the first black woman to receive an Academy Award nomination for Best Actress.

By 1960 the good roles for Dandridge had dried up. She once said, "If I were white, I could capture the world." In 1999 Halle Berry played Dandridge in the movie *Introducing Dorothy Dandridge*. Three years later, Berry became the first African-American woman to win the Oscar for Best Actress, nearly 50 years after Dandridge's nomination.

In the 1950s, Dorothy Dandridge became the toast of Hollywood and was described as one of the most beautiful women in the United States by *Life*. She used her celebrity status as a platform to promote civil rights and organizations such as the NAACP and the National Urban League.

The beauty industry

For much of the late 1800s and 1900s, many cosmetics had been designed to make African Americans more European in appearance. From hair-straightening gels such as "No-Kink," to hot-comb treatments like the "Walker System", and "Dr. Fred Palmer's Skin Whitener," African-American women and men were encouraged to follow white fashion and styles.

In the 1950s, there was a rise in the range of beauty products and treatments for African-American skin and hair. Bleaching creams that altered the shade of a person's skin, and therefore seemed to change a person's heritage, led to conflict within the black community. Despite the **controversy**, African Americans spent millions on these products.

The Johnson Products Company of Chicago, which made products such as "Ultra Wave" and "Afro Sheen" hair straighteners, became the largest African-American-owned manufacturing company in the nation. By the end of the 1960s, annual sales were over $10 million.

Today, hair straightening products are still popular, but African-American women are confidently embracing all features of their beauty. African-American role models like Beyoncé Knowles advertise products for large cosmetics companies while keeping their cultural identity and celebrating their looks.

In the 1920s, African-American women spent hours straightening their hair in an attempt to resemble white styles more closely.

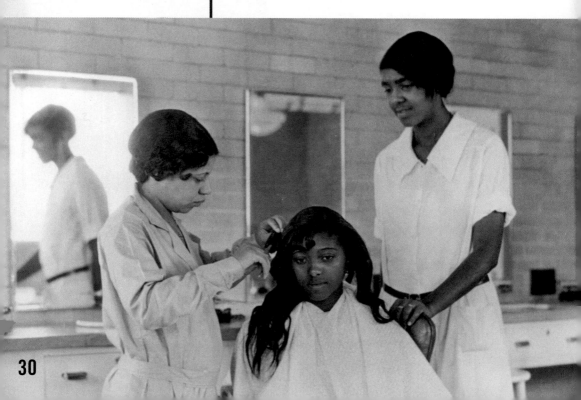

A world apart

In *The Bluest Eye*, Morrison shows the damage that racial **self-loathing** causes. As children, Claudia and her sister have not yet learned to consider that there is anything wrong with them. She looks back on her childhood and says, "We were still in love with ourselves then. We felt comfortable in our skins [...] and could not comprehend this unworthiness." However, Morrison shows that eventually Claudia has her self-love destroyed. Claudia later narrates that in adulthood, she "learned to worship" the white image of beauty, just like everybody else, even though she knows her "worship" is "**fraudulent**."

Despite the growing presence of African-American culture, it was not until the mid-1970s that major cosmetic companies, such as Avon, created a range of products for darker skins.

THE WHITE WAY TO SUCCESS

*Some of the cosmetics advertising that tried to encourage ideas of white beauty in black women used the language of liberation, as though true freedom meant the choice to "be white." The difference in shades of color could mean the difference between economic success or not, and the commercials played on this: "Lighten your dark skin [...] Be attractive. Throw off the chains that have held you back from the **prosperity** that rightly belongs to you."*

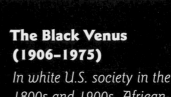

The Black Venus (1906–1975)

In white U.S. society in the 1800s and 1900s, African-American women were often presented in one of two ways: as either primitive **savages** or exotic beauties. However, the 1900s saw the first challenges to white attitudes toward beauty. Josephine Baker was a beautiful African-American dancer, actress, and singer who challenged these **crude** categories. Baker spent much of her professional life performing in Europe, under the name of the Black Venus. In 1925 she performed in Paris at the Théâtre des Champs-Elysées, where she was an instant success, known for her erotic dancing and for appearing practically naked on stage. Playing with white **stereotypes** of the "jungle savage," she performed in a skirt made only of bananas, often accompanied by her pet leopard, Chiquita. The writer Ernest Hemingway called Baker "the most sensational woman anyone ever saw." Baker was so beautiful that she later became the inspiration for many painters and sculptors.

RACIAL PRIDE

Writers and poets of the Harlem Renaissance were trying to turn the tide of negative self-image as early as the 1920s. Writer James Baldwin, made famous for his novel Go Tell It on the Mountain, wrote about identity and race, saying, "You've already been bought and paid for. [...] Now you can love yourself."

The group The Supremes defined the cool, elegant style of young black America in the 1960s and appealed to both black and white audiences. They had a string of top-ten hits and are widely regarded as one of the greatest groups of all time.

Crossover success

By the 1960s, African-American musicians had started to break into new audiences. Sam Cooke was one of the first singers to appeal to black and white audiences in equal measure. Cooke was a pin-up for white and African-American teenagers alike. Despite his early death a few months after the 1964 Civil Right Act was signed, Cooke's fame lived on through his popular racial protest song, "A Change Is Gonna Come." The popularity of African-American music, in particular soul, as exemplified by the hugely successful acts from the **Motown** label, helped form a bridge across racial divisions.

A dangerous desire

The novel's main narrator, Claudia, almost understands what Pecola does not—that the girls cannot achieve the ideal of beauty that they have been taught to crave. She is more **resistant** to white beauty ideals. She is deeply wary of Maureen Peel, who is lighter skinned than she is. Claudia cannot pinpoint why people like Maureen more than her, but she suspects the "thing" that makes Maureen beautiful is her resemblance to whiteness. Claudia's picture books tell her that girls love their white dolls, but she is "physically revolted" by the very thing she is told to adore. When Claudia rejects the white doll she receives for Christmas, she rejects white beauty ideals. Morrison is being **ironic** as Claudia says, "All the world had agreed that a blue-eyed, yellow-haired, pink-skinned doll was what every girl child treasured." Claudia's reaction reflects Morrison's own childhood feelings of being "violently **repelled**" after a black school friend told her she wanted blue eyes.

33

Seeing and being seen

Claudia is able to think beyond the conventions of her community, but Pecola is tied to her small hometown. Morrison has said of small towns, "Most of our lives are spent in little towns [...] And that's where the juices come from and that's where we [are] [...] made who we are." Pecola's life is dramatically affected by the attitudes of her own community. Many in the small-town black community suffer from self-loathing, including her father. This leads to the horror of his sexual assault. Pecola's community lets her down. They do not see the injustice the young girl suffers. Throughout the novel, Pecola is convinced of her unattractiveness and, in her wish to escape the criticism of her community, she becomes "invisible." Morrison describes the young girl as being "concealed, veiled, eclipsed."

When she sees her parents fight, Pecola wants to disappear. In her mind, she imagines that most of her body disappears, but her eyes remain. She has no choice but to see and be seen.

Morrison has described Pecola as a "total and complete victim," whereas Claudia and Frieda have moments of strength. A key difference between the families can be seen when the MacTeer's lodger, Mr. Henry, "picks" at (touches) Frieda when her parents are not at home. Morrison shows us that Frieda could have been sexually abused like Pecola, but instead her parents protect her and chase Mr. Henry out. Frieda is seen, noticed, and then protected. Pecola is ignored.

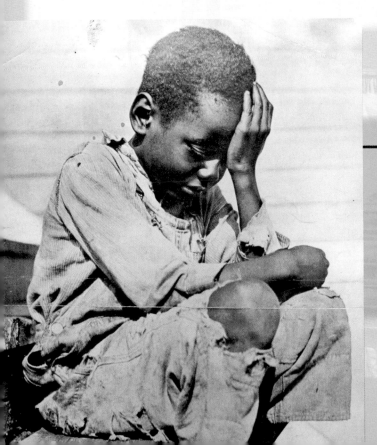

Poverty only contributed to the self-loathing that some African Americans felt within their communities.

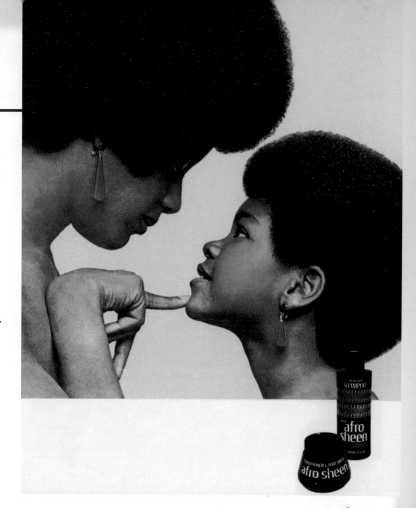

In the 1970s, beauty products for African Americans were linked to a rediscovery of cultural identity. Rather than encouraging black people to adopt white styles, advertisements, such as this one for "Afro Sheen" hair products, focused on black beauty ideals.

Rediscovering identity

After being released from slavery, it was easier for African Americans to survive in U.S. society if their appearance was as close to European as possible. But after more than a century of being told that fair skin, straight hair, and white features were the height of beauty, the African-American community gradually began to recognize and celebrate its own looks.

Twenty years after the terrible events of *The Bluest Eye*, the slogan "black is beautiful" became a **catchphrase** among civil rights groups. Community leaders in the 1960s encouraged African Americans to celebrate their differences from whites and to embrace their own culture. People began adopting beauty styles that emphasized African-American characteristics and heritage, such as the Afro hairstyle. This look emphasizes the different texture of Afro hair, and so highlights the wearer's "differences" from the cultural mainstream.

The Afro became a symbol of black beauty and, by 1965, it was associated with a political statement of black power. By the early 1970s, women's groups were encouraging their members to wear Afros as part of their cultural and gender identity.

Themes, Style, and the Role of the Artist

For Toni Morrison, writing has always been a "way of thinking" and a way of reflecting on experience and creating a point of view. She is interested in the experience and actions of a community already on the outskirts of society. Her novel brings to the center themes, styles of speech, and language that have long been on the edges of society.

The quest

A "quest," or journey, has been a feature of African-American literature since slave stories. The quest is often for freedom, safety, or self-knowledge. Many characters in *The Bluest Eye* are involved in a quest: Pecola for love and an identity; Cholly for his father; Claudia for meaning; and Geraldine for a different social class. Geraldine tries to adopt as many aspects as possible of what she understands to be white culture. She is annoyed with, rather than moved by, Pecola's poverty and disadvantages, saying, "She had seen this little girl all her life [...] Hair uncombed, dresses falling apart." Geraldine's quest for white culture leads her to a cruel disregard toward her own community.

After the Great Depression, unemployment was high. Many African Americans could not provide for their families, and this caused them to lose their sense of purpose. Pecola's father, Cholly, has lost his self-esteem, which has devastating consequences.

A CHILD'S VIEW

Morrison uses the narrative perspective of children to describe adult realities. Claudia and Frieda provide both the voice and the understanding for Pecola's story. The sexual, economic, and social aspects of life are mostly a mystery to them. Their innocence clouds some of the cruelty of Pecola's story, but the reader understands more of the painful truth.

In *The Bluest Eye*, childhood is presented as something the girls have to survive rather than enjoy. Never carefree, Pecola, Claudia, and her sister, Frieda, have daily challenges and threats to cope with, from being teased at school to not having enough to eat.

Attaching blame

Explaining how she framed Pecola's story, Morrison said she created a "series of rejections" that make her an outsider. The most terrible of these is when Pecola is raped by her own father, which then leads to a pregnancy and to the death of her child. This shocking abuse causes Pecola "to literally fall apart" and go insane. At the start of the novel, Morrison's main narrator, Claudia, says, "There is really nothing more to say—except why. But since why is difficult to handle, one must take refuge in how." This means that the focus of the novel is Pecola's destruction, rather than the reasons why it happens. It is only at the very end of the novel that Claudia acknowledges the community itself may have been to blame: Pecola's tragedy is the fault of "the earth, the land, of our town."

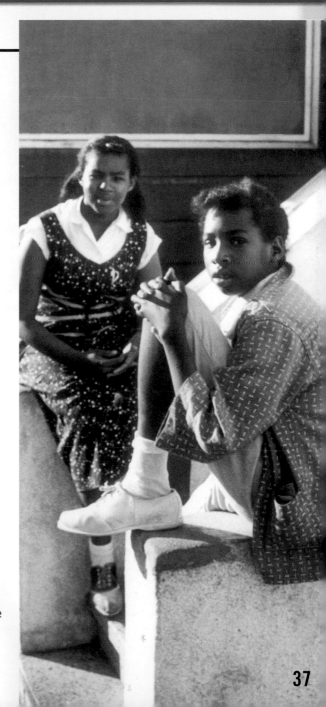

Preachers were central to African-American communities in
the early 1900s. In part of a worldwide meeting of Christians
in Memphis in 1937, a member of the congregation is
touched by a preacher. The meeting was primarily attended
by African Americans from around the world.

Dreams and magic

Faith healers, dream interpreters,
and wise elders were all a part of
African-American communities in
the 1940s. In *The Bluest Eye*, the
characters of Soaphead Church and
M'Dear are important figures within
the African-American community.
They embody various themes,
such as magic, folktales, and the
supernatural. Soaphead Church calls
himself a "Reader, Adviser, and
Interpreter of Dreams." People "find
their way to his door," seeking
help with "anger, yearning, pride,
vengeance, loneliness, misery, defeat,
and hunger." Soaphead gives advice
or help with these matters. Pecola
goes to see Soaphead in an attempt
to get blue eyes.

Another wise figure in the community
is M'Dear. M'Dear is an elderly
woman who serves as a doctor during
Cholly's childhood. She is consulted
on "any illness that could not be
handled by ordinary means." She is
an odd, somewhat isolated figure who
is sometimes **ridiculed**, but she is
never wrong.

Faith in flowers

When the marigolds fail to bloom, the children believe magic is responsible. Claudia, as narrator, tells us that she and Frieda believe they have the power to "change the course of events and alter a human life." They are so convinced of their "own magic" that they believe planting marigolds will save Pecola's baby. Their beliefs are not shaken when Pecola's baby dies. They simply blame each other for the magic's failure.

Soaphead Church is not sorry for his actions or "magic" in giving Pecola the blue eyes she wants. Even though "No one else will see her blue eyes [...] *she* will." Pecola's tragedy is that she will remain overlooked within her own community, noticed only as an object of pity.

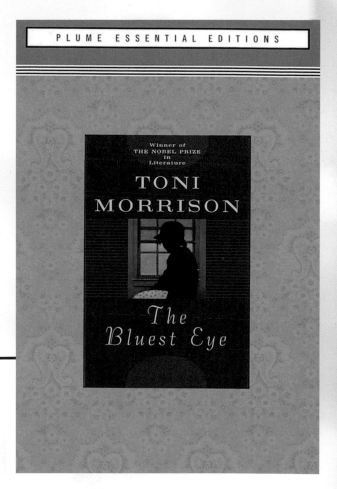

The Bluest Eye has been published with several different covers. Here, in the Plume edition of 1993, the young girl does not look up, preferring to shy away from being seen by the reader.

MONSTROUS PARENTS

Morrison's **Pulitzer Prize**-winning novel, Beloved, published in 1987, is about the haunting of a slave, Sethe, who kills her own baby to prevent her from becoming a slave as well. The distressing subject matter and challenge of recreating the speech and atmosphere of the 1880s made the author think that it might be impossible to write the story. Morrison skilfully manages to capture the horror of Sethe's actions and yet create sympathy for her. In the same way, in The Bluest Eye, Morrison did not want to **dehumanize** the characters who "trashed Pecola and contributed to her collapse." Even though Cholly rapes his own daughter, there is a measure of understanding that he, too, has suffered. His crime is unforgivable, but it has its roots in the cruelty Cholly himself has suffered.

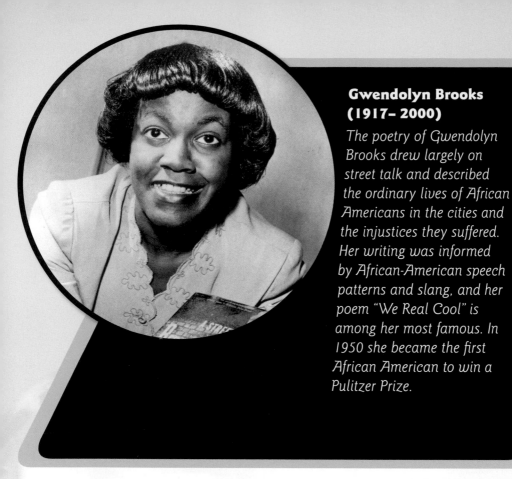

The language of speech

Like many of Morrison's works, *The Bluest Eye* has a "broken narrative" that the reader must put together. The novel begins by breaking down a paragraph from a school reading book, gradually taking away the punctuation and removing the visual structures of written language.

The opening phrase "quiet as it's kept" announces something that Morrison calls "a silence broken, a void filled, an unspeakable thing spoken at last." It invites the reader to listen to the story to find out what the secret is. Morrison has described the style of narration and relationship with the reader as a "secret being shared." Actually, Pecola's intimate story is made public through the closeness of the community, which is the very same community that shuns her and, in Morrison's own words, "condemned her." The main part of the novel is presented by different narrators, and so Pecola's story is seen from different perspectives.

In the novel, Morrison wanted to create a language "worthy" of African-American speech. Following the oral tradition of storytelling and African-American writers, such as Gwendolyn Brooks, Morrison wants her writing to sound like real speech, a style known as **aural literature**.

Audience participation

In African-American churches in the 1800s, few people could read, and so preachers repeated words, phrases, and common expressions, and the audience would respond by joining in on the repetitions. This style of preaching meant the audience was actively engaged in the worship. In a similar way, Morrison wants the reader to participate in her novels. In *Beloved*, she uses the model of the African-American preacher. Baby Suggs is a former slave who is a spiritual elder of the community. She draws people to a religious gathering in a clearing in the woods. In this 1880s outside church, she preaches a powerful sermon, repeating words for emphasis and to include the crowd's responses: "We flesh; flesh that weeps, laughs; flesh that dances on bare feet in grass. Love it. Love it hard [...] *You* got to love it, *you*!" Like the main theme in *The Bluest Eye*, the message here is to have pride and love yourself, because a wider, racist society may not. In all her novels, Morrison wants "to restore the language that black people spoke to its original power."

Morrison uses her profile to raise issues of concern for the African-American community. Here, she makes an appearance on *The Oprah Winfrey Show*, in October 1996.

Women and family

Many of Morrison's novels deal with issues of social status, economic and political factors, and cultural heritage. Within the framework of a community, she is most interested in African-American women, their experience, and their roles.

In her second novel, *Sula* (1973), it is female friendships and the choices women make that are the main issues. A quest for cultural identity is the basis for *Song of Solomon* (1977), and supernatural and emotional dilemmas are central to the story of *Beloved*. Her novel *Paradise* (1997) shows how a community turns on itself, and *Love* (2003) examines the effects of integration on the black community.

Fragile beauty

On the issue of self-loathing, Morrison believes "a lot has changed since the 1960s in terms of self-image. But there's still a lot of pain young girls feel because the bar is always being raised." Morrison believes that African Americans began to reclaim their racial beauty in the 1960s, and this prompted not only her story, but also a new celebration of African-American culture. This is in direct contrast to the situation in 1941 in *The Bluest Eye*. Here, whiteness is "the norm," and Pecola and others in her community are vulnerable to the idea that it is superior. Morrison has spoken of the young girl's descent into madness, explaining that Pecola had no choice. To escape the horror of her life, Pecola "made a door for herself. And that was her insanity."

Today, many African-Americans celebrate black culture. Beyoncé Knowles is a worldwide superstar, famous for her singing, acting, and commercials for hair and beauty products. She is seen here at the 46th annual Grammy Awards, 2004, where she won a record five awards for her contributions to music. Knowles's five awards tied a record set by Alicia Keys, Norah Jones, and Lauryn Hill—other black and mixed-race artists— for the most Grammys won by a female artist.

From the mid-1800s to the present day, the process of making a quilt has been an important social activity for women of all ages across the United States. As people sewed, stories would be told, problems advised upon, and neighborhood issues discussed.

A patchwork quilt

The economic migration north in the early 1940s broke up settled communities. In the novel, Pauline and Cholly remove themselves from their families and the community they know. Morrison uses the image of a patchwork quilt to explain the effect of this removal on the Breedlove family. The image of the quilt is usually a unifying one, where different people come together to produce a whole.

The preacher and politician Jesse Jackson has used this **metaphor** many times to explain the rich variety within the U.S. population:

> *America is not like a blanket [...] America is more like a quilt: many patches, many pieces, many colors, many sizes, all woven and held together by a common thread.*

In contrast, Morrison uses the image of the quilt to explain the Breedlove family's absolute isolation from each other. Their family unit has been broken down through grinding poverty, migration, and a reinforced belief that they are unworthy of love—"Each member of the family [...] making his own patchwork quilt of reality." Through making their own symbolic quilt-squares of separate lives, the break up of the family continues.

In 1992 Toni Morrison said, "I am really Chloe Anthony Wofford. That's who I am. I have been writing under this other person's name." The author has said she regrets having called herself Toni Morrison when *The Bluest Eye* was published in 1970. Her own search for an identity reflects the larger issue within the African-American community.

For Morrison, black women, their identities, and their worlds were overlooked in both real life and literature before the civil rights movement. She wrote her novel because she "wanted to read it" and to tell a story about people she could identify with. Although *The Bluest Eye* was praised, Morrison believes that it was at first "misread [...] just like Pecola's life." The sensitive subject matter and the groundbreaking writing style meant that it was controversial and not a best-seller. Morrison kept her editing job and continued to write novels in the evenings. Her second novel, *Sula*, earned greater acclaim, but it was with her third novel, *Song of Solomon*, published in 1977, that her literary greatness was finally recognized when she won the National Book Critics Circle Award.

In March 1981, Morrison was featured on the cover of *Newsweek*. She was the first African-American woman to appear on the cover since Zora Neale Hurston in 1943. She has also been featured on the cover of *Time* magazine, (seen left).

When her novel Beloved failed to win the 1987 National Book Award, Morrison's fellow writers were outraged. They believed that the novel was so masterful that it clearly deserved to win. An open letter signed by 48 prominent black writers, including Maya Angelou and Alice Walker, was published in the New York Times Book Review in January of that year. The writers protested that Morrison's achievements had not been suitably recognized or celebrated. In 1988 Beloved won the Pulitzer Prize.

Eyes on the prize

Gradually Morrison's works drew praise from readers and critics around the world who recognized a powerful individual voice. In 1993 she became only the eighth woman to be awarded the Nobel Prize for Literature. The awarding committee said that Morrison's novels gave "life to an essential aspect of American reality," freeing language from the "**fetters** of race."

Phillis Wheatley (1753–1784) and other voices of slavery

The first prominent African-American author was the poet Phillis Wheatley. Born in Senegal, Africa, Wheatley was captured and sold into slavery at the age of seven. Her Poems on Various Subjects *of 1773 drew high praise, including from George Washington, for whom she composed a poem. In the 1800s, many former slaves wrote narratives to expose the true reality of slave life. The* Narrative of the Life of Frederick Douglass, an American Slave *was a best-seller in 1845. The white, liberal writer Harriet Beecher Stowe wrote an 1852 fictional account of the horrors of slavery,* Uncle Tom's Cabin. *This was one of the most popular and widely read books of its time. Following this tradition, Morrison's* Beloved *is based on a true story of a runaway slave.*

Powerful female voices

In 1987 Morrison said that she realized a "renaissance" had taken place in African-American women's writing. Initially popular and fashionable during the civil rights movement, African-American women writers have made a powerful impression on U.S. and global culture from the 1930s to the present day. Telling stories of what it is to be both black and female, these writers have continued a rich tradition of African-American storytelling that began in slave narratives and continues today across a range of media.

One of the earliest best-sellers by an African-American woman was the 1937 novel *Their Eyes Were Watching God*, by Zora Neale Hurston. It is about a young black woman named Janie who struggles to find a place for herself within the strict confines of a small southern town. Hurston shows black women and their experience through the small-town society's treatment of Janie.

In *The Bluest Eye*, Claudia has yet to realize the restrictions imposed upon her. She says, "Our limitations were not known to us—not then." This implies that she may in time learn what Hurston's Janie comes to know—that because of her gender and race, her opportunities are limited.

Maya Angelou (1928–)

Writer, actress, and civil rights activist Maya Angelou is considered one of the great voices of contemporary American Literature. Her most famous book is I Know Why the Caged Bird Sings *(1969), which is the first part of a multi-volume autobiography. It charts her childhood rape and her struggle to overcome this trauma. To support her young son, Angelou danced in nightclubs, cooked at a Creole café, and removed paint in a car repair shop. In the 1960s, she worked for Martin Luther King Jr. and his Southern Christian Leadership Conference. Angelou's work tries to bridge racial divisions and celebrate the good things, or "rainbows," in life.*

The female perspective

Alice Walker is one of the United States' most distinguished writers. She shares Hurston's and Morrison's concerns about the treatment of African-American women in society. Born in Georgia in 1944 to a family of sharecroppers, she was a scholarship student at Spelman College, a historically black liberal arts college for women in Atlanta, Georgia. She returned to live in Mississippi and was active in the civil rights movement of the 1960s.

She has campaigned for women's issues and the **anti-apartheid** movement. In 1983 she won both the Pulitzer Prize and the National Book Award for her novel *The Color Purple*. A book written in the form of letters, *The Color Purple* tells the story of Celie, a young woman who is sexually abused by her father and is then forced to marry a man who physically abuses her. The novel was later made into a movie by Steven Spielberg.

Alice Walker is seen here in 1985, two years after winning the Pulitzer Prize and the National Book Award for her novel *The Color Purple*. Walker is widely respected for being outspoken about her views, regardless of the popular public opinions at the time.

A search for love and identity

More than 30 years after its publication, *The Bluest Eye* remains an important and confronting work. The novel's central concerns of racial segregation, inequality of opportunity, and loss of identity are still relevant today. In October 1995, hundreds of thousands of African Americans rallied in Washington, D.C., to take part in the Million Man March. The march was aimed at encouraging African-American men to improve their families and communities. Many of the crowd voiced their anger at what they perceived as the unequal treatment of African Americans. The United States has achieved significant progress, but there is still work to be done before true racial equality exists. Until this happens, Pecola and the Breedloves' haunting story will remain powerfully relevant.

The proof of progress

Today, there is greater economic equality, and African Americans hold positions of power in every walk of U.S. life. African-American supermodels grace the catwalks and black actresses are praised for their performances. In the arts, particularly, there are many more African-American role models for young people to look up to. Through influential voices like Morrison's, more black writers are exploring their experiences and adding to the wealth of African-American literature.

After years of makeup artists not knowing what colors to use on her, the Somali-born supermodel, Iman, was one of the first women to launch a range of makeup suitable for black skin.

In 1989 Morrison became the first African American to hold a professor's chair at an Ivy League university when she became the Robert F. Goheen Professor in the Humanities Council at Princeton University.

Journalists and reviewers have sometimes criticized Morrison for being too political in her work. These critics, however, are in the minority. Most readers marvel at her ability to join together story, history, and gender issues and express them within the language of written speech. Her work has reached a large, multi-ethnic readership.

A lasting hunger

Morrison thinks that a characteristic of African-American writers is a "quality of hunger and disturbance that never ends." By this, she means that the quest for identity, equality, and social and political justice goes on. Morrison's writings present freedom as a choice, which brings with it responsibilities.

In December 2000, Morrison was honored as a National Humanities Medalist for work that "celebrated our **diversity**, tested our beliefs and connected us to each other and our common **humanity**." In an interview after her novel *Love* was published in 2003, Morrison reflected on her body of work, saying, "I was always interested in efforts people make to thrive, to survive, and to relate to one another." This has been at the heart of Morrison's work from her first novel, and is central to Pecola's story. As Morrison herself explains, "The search for love and identity runs through most everything I write."

TIME LINE

1863	Emancipation Proclamation is signed January 1, ending slavery.
1870s	Various civil rights acts are passed but disputed and largely ignored (called the Reconstruction Era).
1918	Harlem Renaissance begins.
1929	Wall Street Crash and start of the Great Depression.
1931	On February 18, Chloe Anthony Wofford is born in Lorain, Ohio.
1941	Japanese attack on Pearl Harbor. The U.S. enters World War II.
1941	Pecola's story, *The Bluest Eye*, is set in this year.
1949	Chloe Wofford goes to Howard University and changes her name to Toni.
1953	After receiving a B.A., Toni Wofford goes to Cornell University for graduate studies in English literature.
1954	U.S. Supreme Court rules school segregation unconstitutional.
1955	Wofford goes to Texas Southern University in Houston to teach English and the humanities.
1955	Rosa Parks refuses to give up her seat on a city bus to a white passenger and is arrested. Segregation in public parks and playgrounds is banned.
1956	After a year of protest, buses are integrated in Montgomery.
1957	Toni Wofford returns to teach at Howard.
1957	President Dwight D. Eisenhower orders federal troops to enforce school desegregation in Little Rock, Arkansas.
1958	Toni Wofford marries Jamaican architect Harold Morrison.
1960	Four black students sit at a "whites only" lunch counter in a school in North Carolina.
1961	Freedom Riders are attacked in Alabama.
1961	Morrison's son (Harold) Ford is born.
1962	Morrison joins a writer's group and meets Claude Brown; she writes a short story that will become *The Bluest Eye*.
1962	James Meredith is the first African American to enroll at the University of Mississippi.
1963	Civil rights leader Medgar Evers is shot and killed in Jackson, Mississippi. Two months later, more than 200,000 Americans March on Washington, D.C., for civil rights.

KEY	Local/national history (United States)
	Author's life
	The Bluest Eye

1964	Toni and Harold Morrison are divorced. Son Slade is born.
1964	President Lyndon B. Johnson signs the Civil Rights Act. Martin Luther King Jr. wins the Nobel Peace Prize.
1965	Morrison begins work on *The Bluest Eye*.
1965	Voting Rights Act is passed.
1967	Thurgood Marshall is sworn in as the first black Supreme Court justice.
1968	King is assassinated in Memphis, Tennessee.
1970	*The Bluest Eye* is published.
1973	*Sula* is published.
1975–1978	Morrison teaches at Yale University.
1977	*Song of Solomon* is published.
1978	Morrison is named as Distinguished Writer of 1978 by the American Academy of Arts and Letters.
1980	President Jimmy Carter appoints Morrison to the National Council on the Arts.
1981	*Tar Baby* is published. Morrison is elected to the Writer's Guild and the Author's League.
1984	Morrison accepts the Albert Schweitzer Professorship of the Humanities at the State University of New York at Albany.
1987	*Beloved* is published. Morrison becomes the Regent's Lecturer at the University of California, Berkeley.
1988	Morrison is elected to the American Academy of Arts and Letters. *Beloved* wins the Pulitzer Prize for Fiction.
1989	Morrison accepts the Robert Goheen Professorship in the Humanities Council at Princeton University. The joint appointment is in African American Studies and Creative Writing.
1992	*Jazz* and a collection of essays, *Playing in the Dark: Whiteness and the Literary Imagination*, are published.
1992	Race riots in Los Angeles after police assault an African-American man named Rodney King.
1993	Morrison wins the Nobel Prize for Literature.
1998	*Paradise*, Morrison's seventh novel, is published.
2003	*Love*, Morrison's eighth novel, is published.

The edition of *The Bluest Eye* used in the writing of this book was published by Vintage, London, in 1999.

Other works by Toni Morrison

Novels

The Bluest Eye. Holt, Rinehart, and Winston, 1970
Sula. New York: Alfred A. Knopf, 1973.
Song of Solomon. New York: Alfred A. Knopf, 1977.
Tar Baby. New York: Alfred A. Knopf, 1981.
Beloved. New York: Alfred A. Knopf, 1987.
Jazz. New York: Alfred A. Knopf, 1992.
Paradise. New York: Alfred A. Knopf, 1998.
Love. New York: Alfred A. Knopf, 2003.

Plays/Operas

Dreaming Emmett, 1986.
New Orleans, 1983.

Children's books (with son Slade Morrison)

The Big Box. New York: Hyperion Books for Children, 1999.

Further reading

Beecher Stowe, Harriet. *Uncle Tom's Cabin.* New York: Barnes & Noble, 2003.

Bridges, Ruby. *Through My Eyes.* New York: Scholastic, 1999.

Holliday, Laurel, ed. *Dreaming in Color: Living in Black And White.* New York: Pocket, 2000.

Levine, Ellen, ed. *Freedom's Children: Young Civil Rights Activists Tell Their Own Stories.* New York: Puffin, 2000.

Neale Hurston, Zora. *Their Eyes Were Watching God.* New York: HarperCollins, 2000.

Walker, Alice. *The Color Purple.* Orlando, Fla.: Harcourt, 2003.

Movies

Amistad (1997). Directed by Stephen Spielberg.

Beloved (1998). Directed by Jonathan Demme.

Separate but Equal (1991). Directed by George Stevens Jr.

Places to visit

African American Museum, 1765 Crawford Road, Cleveland, Ohio 44106

Birmingham Civil Rights Institute, 520 Sixteenth Street North, Birmingham, Alabama 35203

National Civil Rights Museum, 450 Mulberry Street, Memphis, Tenn. 38103

Websites

African American Museum: www.aamcleveland.org

Birmingham Civil Rights Institute: www.bcri.org

National Civil Rights Museum: www.civilrightsmuseum.org

Southern Christian Leadership Conference: sclcnational.org

The Toni Morrison Society website: www.tonimorrisonsociety.org

The National Association for the Advancement of Colored People: www.naacp.org

GLOSSARY

activist campaigner or protester

afterword concluding section in a book

allegation unproved accusation of wrongdoing

alliance relationship based on shared values or for mutual benefit

anti-apartheid against a political system that separates people according to their race

aristocrat member of the aristocracy, a class of society made up of people of noble birth

aural literature writing that recreates the sounds of spoken language

autobiography account of a person's life written by that person

boycott withdraw from business or relations with someone as a protest

burlap sack coarse canvas bag

catchphrase well-known sentence or phrase

Civil Rights Act landmark legislation passed on July 2, 1964, that outlawed discrimination based on race, color, religion, sex, or national origin

color-line barrier between different races

congregation group of worshippers

controversy topic causing strong disagreement

crude offensively coarse or rude

curfew official time after which people have to remain indoors at night

dehumanize make someone seem less human

demonization to make somebody appear evil or wicked

devalue reduce or underestimate the worth or importance of something

discontent unhappiness

discrimination making an unjust decision in the treatment of a person or group based on race, sex, or age

disempower make less powerful

displace move from the proper or usual position

diversity state of being widely varied

empower give someone confidence

faun young deer in its first year

fetters chains or shackles

fraudulent deceitful or dishonest

gender state of being male or female

Great Depression name given to the economic crisis in the United States that lasted from 1929 to 1939

grotesque distorted in a strange or disturbing way

hallucinate imagine something that is not actually there

humanity qualities of a human being

ideal perfect example

immigrant person who comes to live in a new country

impoverished made poor

incest sexual relations between close relatives

integration to come into equal participation in a group

internalize make attitudes or behavior part of one's nature through learning

ironic happening in the opposite way from what is expected and causing amusement because of it

Ku Klux Klan (KKK) southern white racist terrorist group formed in 1866 to fight for white supremacy

landlord someone who leases land or property

lynch to seize somebody suspected of a crime and kill him or her, usually by hanging

mainstream normal or conventional ideas, attitudes, or activities

metaphor thing regarded as symbolic of something else

migrate move from place to place, often in order to find work

momentum driving force gained by the development of a process

Motown soul music released on the Detroit record label Motown Records

myth widely held but false belief

narrative spoken or written account of events; a story

National Association for the Advancement of Colored People (NAACP) one of the oldest and most influential civil rights organizations in the United States. It was founded February 12, 1909, to work on behalf of African Americans.

Nazi Party National Socialist German Worker's Party, which came to power during the 1930s under Adolf Hitler

Nobel Prize annual international award for outstanding contributions to society in various categories

perception how things are seen or regarded

persecution subjecting someone to prolonged hostility and ill-treatment

plantation large estate on which crops such as coffee, sugar, and tobacco are grown

prejudice opinion that is not based on reason or actual experience; unjust behavior formed on such a basis

primer book used for teaching reading

prosperity success, wealth

prudent acting with or showing care and thought for the future

Pulitzer Prize award in the U.S. for outstanding artistic achievement in literature, music, or journalism

quest long, hard search

rape force somebody to have sexual intercourse against his or her will

repel to be repulsive or distasteful to

renaissance revival or renewed interest in something

resistant withstanding the action or effect of something

ridicule mockery or making fun of

saturate dominate or drench

savage primitive or uncivilized

segregate separate along racial, sexual, or religious lines

self-loathing hatred of oneself

sharecropper tenant farmer who farms land for the owner and is paid a share of the value of the harvested crop

sharecropping farming land as a sharecropper

soliloquy act of speaking one's thoughts aloud when alone

stark severe or bare in appearance; harsh

stereotype oversimplified image of a person or group of people

Student Nonviolent Coordinating Committee group that emerged in 1960 as a major institution of the civil rights movement. It coordinated the use of nonviolent direct action to attack segregation and other forms of racism.

supremacy superiority

unalienable unchangeable, undeniable

vengeance revenge

Voting Rights Act law that outlawed the requirement that would-be voters take literacy (reading and writing) tests to qualify to register to vote. It provided for federal registration of voters.

vulnerable exposed to attack or harm

Wall Street Crash stock-market crash of late October 1929, when share prices on the New York Stock Exchange collapsed

workhouse jail where offenders are expected to work

INDEX